First World War
and Army of Occupation
War Diary
France, Belgium and Germany

58 DIVISION
175 Infantry Brigade
215 Machine Gun Company
9 September 1915 - 30 January 1918

WO95/3009/11

The Naval & Military Press Ltd
www.nmarchive.com
Published in association with The National Archives

Published by

The Naval & Military Press Ltd

Unit 10 Ridgewood Industrial Park,
Uckfield, East Sussex,
TN22 5QE England
Tel: +44 (0) 1825 749494

www.naval-military-press.com

www.nmarchive.com

This diary has been reprinted in facsimile from the original. Any imperfections are inevitably reproduced and the quality may fall short of modern type and cartographic standards.

© Crown Copyright
Images reproduced by permission of The National Archives, London, England, 2015.

Contents

Document type	Place/Title	Date From	Date To
Heading	WO95/3009/9		
Heading	The Officer Commanding 2/12th Battn. London Regt.		
War Diary	Woodbridge	09/09/1915	28/09/1915
War Diary	Woodbridge	05/10/1915	12/02/1916
Heading	WO95/3009/10		
Heading	War Diary Of 2/12th London Regt.		
War Diary	Long Bridge Deverill	04/01/1917	04/01/1917
War Diary	Warminster	05/02/1917	05/02/1917
War Diary	Southampton	05/02/1917	05/02/1917
War Diary	Havre	06/02/1917	07/02/1917
War Diary	Auxi-Le-Chateaux	08/02/1917	08/02/1917
War Diary	Wavans	09/02/1917	10/02/1917
War Diary	Beaudricourt	11/02/1917	14/02/1917
War Diary	Halloy	19/02/1917	27/02/1917
Heading	War Diary Of 2/12th London ("The Rangers") From February 28th 1917 To March 26th 1917 Volume 1		
War Diary	Halloy	28/02/1917	01/03/1917
War Diary	Hallo to Bailleulval	02/03/1917	03/03/1917
War Diary	Bailleulval	04/03/1917	04/03/1917
War Diary	Wailly	05/03/1917	07/03/1917
War Diary	Wailly (Sector F2)	08/03/1917	19/03/1917
War Diary	Ficheux	20/03/1917	26/03/1917
Heading	War Diary Of 2/12 London Regt (The Rangers) From March 27th To April 26th 1917 Volume I		
War Diary	Halloy	27/03/1917	01/04/1917
War Diary	Neuvillette	02/04/1917	02/04/1917
War Diary	Noeux	03/04/1917	05/04/1917
War Diary	Busles Artois	06/04/1917	06/04/1917
War Diary	Miraumont	08/04/1917	09/04/1917
War Diary	Achiet Le Petit	10/04/1917	26/04/1917
Heading	War Diary Of 2/12th. Bn. Ldn. Regt. (The Rangers). From 27th. April 1917 To 27th. May 1917 Volume 4		
War Diary	Achiet Le Petit	27/04/1917	15/05/1917
War Diary	Bihucourt	16/05/1917	27/05/1917
Heading	War Diary Of 2/12 London (The Rangers) From May 30th To June 30th 1917 Vol. 5		
War Diary	Night of	28/05/1917	23/06/1917
War Diary	Mory	24/06/1917	25/06/1917
Heading	War Diary Of 2/12th London Regt. (The Rangers) From June 25th 1917 To July 31st 1917 Vol. VI		
War Diary	Logeast Wood	25/06/1917	08/07/1917
War Diary	Havrincourt Wood	08/07/1917	22/07/1917
War Diary	Night of	23/07/1917	24/07/1917
War Diary	Ruyaulcourt	23/07/1917	26/07/1917
War Diary	Bertincourt	27/07/1917	27/07/1917
War Diary	Daineville	27/07/1917	31/07/1917
Heading	War Diary Of 2/12th. London (The Rangers) From August 1st To August 31st 1917 Vol. 7		
War Diary	Dainville	01/08/1917	19/08/1917
War Diary	Night of	24/08/1917	13/09/1917

War Diary	Ypres Canal	13/09/1917	30/09/1917
Heading	War Diary 2/12th Bn. London Regt. October 1917 Volume I		
War Diary		01/10/1917	08/10/1917
War Diary	Zutkerque	01/10/1917	30/10/1917
Heading	War Diary 2/12th London Regiment (The Rangers) November 1917		
War Diary	Kempton Park N.W. Of Ypres	31/10/1917	14/11/1917
War Diary	Proven	15/11/1917	30/11/1917
War Diary	Seninghem & Affringues	01/12/1917	13/12/1917
War Diary	Poelcappelle	12/12/1917	31/12/1917
Heading	War Diary 12th Bn (Late 2/12th) Bn. London Regt. From January 1st 1918 To January 31st 1918 Volume I		
War Diary	Kempton Pk.	01/01/1918	06/01/1918
War Diary	Herzeele	07/01/1918	30/01/1918

WO 95
3009/9

From

The Officer Commanding 2/12th Battn. London Regt.

To

Head Quarters
175th Infantry Brigade

Monthly Statement in Connection with War Diary.

No Remarks

Arthur S Bastow
Col.
Comdg. 2/12th Bn. London Regt.

Woodbridge
31 August 1915.

WAR DIARY or INTELLIGENCE SUMMARY

Army Form C. 2118.

BATTALION 12th LONDON REGIMENT, "THE RANGERS,"

MONTH OF SEPTEMBER 1915.

(Erase heading not required.)

Instructions regarding War Diaries and the Staff Manual respectively will be prepared in manuscript.

Hour, Date, Place	Summary of Events and Information	Remarks and references to Appendices
2 a.m. 9th. Sept. 1915. WOODBRIDGE.	8 p.m. 8th. Sept. Battalion ordered from Brigade H.Q. to take up anti-aircraft positions. 2 a.m. 9th. Sept. troops withdrawn No aircraft seen or heard.	
12.45 a.m. 10th. Sept. 15.	8.15 p.m. 9th. Sept. Order from Bde. H.Q. to take up anti-aircraft positions. 12.35 a.m. 10th. Sept. Troops ordered to return to Camp but remain ready at short notice. No aircraft seen or heard.	
2.25 a.m. 12th. Sept. 15.	9115 p.m. 11th. Sept. Troops ordered to stand by in Camp. 10.23 p.m. Positions ordered to be taken up. 2.25 a.m. 12th. Sepr. Troops withdrawn. No aircraft seen or heard.	
1.20 a.m. 13th. Sept. 15.	11.53 p.m. 12th. Sept. Order to stand by received from Bde. H.Q. 11.53 p.m. to 12 midnight 12/13 Septr. Zeppelin heard & seen & passed right overhead from S.W. to N.E. This was reported to Brigade. The vessel was flying at a great height and there was no firing. A rocket was seen due E. Magnetic from the Camp was reported to Brigade Headquarters. 1.20 a.m. Troops returned to quarters.	
2.30 a.m. 14th. Septr. 1915.	7.30 p.m. 13th. Sept. Orders received to take up anti-aircraft positions. 12 midnight 13/14 Sept. Zeppelin heard to S.W. and passed away to S.E. dropping several bombs en route, gunfire also heard. The vessel last heard 12.20 a.m. 14th. Sept. 1915. Report sent to Brigade 12.30 a.m. 14th. Sept. Troops returned to Camp 2 a.m. 14th. September.	

Army Form C. 2118.

WAR DIARY
or
INTELLIGENCE SUMMARY.

(Erase heading not required.)

BATTALION 12th LONDON REGIMENT, "THE RANGERS."

Instructions regarding War Diaries and Intelligence Summaries are contained in F. S. Regs., Part II. and the Staff Manual respectively. Title pages will be prepared in manuscript.

Hour, Date, Place	Summary of Events and Information	Remarks and references to Appendices
1.10 a.m. 16th. Sepr. 15	8.8 p.m. 15th. Septr. Order from Brigade to take up anti-aircraft positions. 1.3 a.m. 16th. September Troops ordered to returned to Camp No aircraft seen or heard.	
18th. Sept. 1915.	Inspection of Camp by Brigadier.	
7.15 p.m. 18th. Sep. 15.	Period of Vigilance commences.	
3.30 p.m. 19th. Sept. 15	Period of Vigilance ends.	
28th. Sept. 1915.	Section of trenches aloted to 175th. Brigade between R. DEBEN & G. of MAIDENSGRAVE 1" Ord. Map. 2/12th. Battalion is to take left section of this.	

Colonel,

Commanding 2nd. Battalion, "The Rangers" The 12th. London Regiment.

Army Form C. 2118.

WAR DIARY
or
INTELLIGENCE SUMMARY
(Erase heading not required.)

October 1915

Stamp: 3 - NOV 1915 LONDON DIVISION GENERAL STAFF

Hour, Date, Place	Summary of Events and Information	Remarks and references to Appendices
12:35am 5th October 1915 Woodbridge	10.20 p.m. 4th October warning received to prepare for aircraft action. 10.10 p.m. Order received to take up positions. 12.35 a.m. 5th Oct. Troops ordered to return to camp. N.C.O. in charge of motor observation post reports: airship to E travelling ESE very low. No other reports. Cloudy high.	
3 a.m. 14th October 1915	7.20 p.m. October 19th 1915 order ordered to take up aircraft positions at once. 8.47 p.m. 12 gunshots heard to NE by No 3 post (C Coy). 11.10 p.m. Zeppelin heard by all outpost Coys & also by Bn. H.Q. machine gun rifle & gun fire heard. No fort of this Battn. was able to fire as nothing was seen. The aircraft proceeded NE.	

Army Form C. 2118.

WAR DIARY
or
INTELLIGENCE SUMMARY

(Erase heading not required.)

Instructions regarding War Diaries and Intelligence Summaries are contained in F. S. Regs., Part II. and the Staff Manual respectively. Title pages will be prepared in manuscript.

Hour, Date, Place	Summary of Events and Information	Remarks and references to Appendices
3 am 14th October 1915 continued	1.10 am 14th Oct. Zeppelin heard SW & another to NW - the first three was reported by No 4 post & second by No 3 post - both seen shortly Bn HQ. Troops returned to camp 3 a.m.	CH.
6 pm 15th October 1915 Woodbridge	The bat left Grove Farm Huts, Woodbridge & occupied billets in the town. Bn HQ established at Deben Gate.	CH.
3.30 pm 19th October 1915 Woodbridge	10.45 am. order received to be prepared to take up Anti-aircraft positions. 3.30 pm. "Resume Normal" message received.	CH.
12 midnight 27/28 October 1915 Woodbridge	8.40 pm. order received stand by for aircraft action. 9.20 pm. Positions taken up, except MG which was away at Ipswich. 11.45 pm. Troops ordered into camp.	CH.

Arthur S Parker Col.
(Comdg 2/12th Bn London Regt.)

WAR DIARY

INTELLIGENCE SUMMARY
(Erase heading not required.)

Army Form C. 2118.

November 1915

Hour, Date, Place	Summary of Events and Information	Remarks and references to Appendices
8 p.m. 8th November 1915 Woodbridge	Warning received to take anti-aircraft action. Positions taken up accordingly. No aircraft either seen or heard.	C.H.
27th November 1915 Woodbridge	In compliance with W/O letters referring strengths of Officers to 23. The following Officers detailed to proceed C.H. to return 2/12th p.m. Major Tucker, 2/Lt Wall-Row, Telfer, Harl, Janisch; 2/Lt Galbraith, to proceed in return of Lieut Howard. Capt Webster awaits decision of Medical Board. Lieut Anstice is borne on strength for extra-regimental duty.	C.H.

Arthur S Balmer
Col Comdg
2/12 Rhodesian Regt.

WAR DIARY
INTELLIGENCE SUMMARY.
(Erase heading not required.)

Army Form C. 2118.

Month of December 1915.

Place	Date	Hour	Summary of Events and Information	Remarks and references to Appendices
Woodbridge	2/12/15	5/pm	Section of position to be held in case of enemy landing allotted to 2/12 Bn. to Worth upon near Goldbrook Hall.	CM.
"	9/12/15		Capt E F Webster transferred to 102nd Provisional Bn.	CM.
"	15/12/15		Warning received the needs to moved shot notice to Aldershot.	CM.
"	19/12/15	6/pm	Sentry over Bn HQ reports hearing aircraft.	
"		9:30/pm	Message from Brigade HQ to effect that aircraft was British aeroplane	CM.
"	31/12/15		Inspection of Division by G.O.C.	

Arthur S Davham
Col. comdg.
2/12 Bn London Regt.

Army Form C. 2118.

WAR DIARY 2/12 Bn London Regt.

INTELLIGENCE SUMMARY.

January 1916

(Erase heading not required.)

Instructions regarding War Diaries and Intelligence Summaries are contained in F. S. Regs., Part II. and the Staff Manual respectively. Title pages will be prepared in manuscript.

Place	Date	Hour	Summary of Events and Information	Remarks and references to Appendices
Woodbridge	3rd Jan 1916	5pm	56 Expeditionary Force men transferred to 3/12th Bn London Regt.	CH
"	4th Jan	5pm	57 recruits from 3/12th Bn London Regt taken on strength.	CH
"	13th Jan	6pm	2nd Lieut H.D. PEABODY arrives from 3/12th Bn Ldn Regt.	CH
"	15th/27th Jan	6pm	2nd Lieut L W HART returned from 3/12th Bn Ldn Regt.	CH
"	31st		31 recruits under the group system taken on strength.	CH
"	22nd	6pm	20 recruits " " " " " "	CH
"	24th	6pm	31 recruits " " " " " "	CH
"	25th	6pm	38 recruits " " " " " "	CH
"	26th	6pm	23 recruits " " " " " "	CH
"	27th	6pm	16 recruits " " " " " "	CH
"	28th	6pm	16 recruits " " " " " "	CH
"	29th	6pm	15 recruits " " " " " "	CH
"	31st	6pm	16 recruits " " " " " "	CH

Clive Hardy Capt & adjt.
for Col comdg.
2/12 Bn London Regt.

Army Form C. 2118.

WAR DIARY

INTELLIGENCE SUMMARY.

for February 1916

2/12 Bn London Regt.

(Erase heading not required.)

Instructions regarding War Diaries and Intelligence Summaries are contained in F. S. Regs., Part II. and the Staff Manual respectively. Title pages will be prepared in manuscript.

Place	Date	Hour	Summary of Events and Information	Remarks and references to Appendices
Woodbridge	1st Feb 1916	6 pm	14 recruits under Group system taken on strength	CH
"	2nd Feb	6 pm	51 recruits under Group system taken on strength	CH
"	3rd Feb	6 pm	26 recruits under Group system taken on strength	CH
"	9th Feb	6 pm	43 recruits under Group system taken on strength	CH
"	10th Feb	6 pm	30 recruits under Group system taken on strength	CH
"	11th Feb	6 pm	16 recruits under Group system taken on strength	CH
"	12th Feb	6 pm	51 recruits under Group system taken on strength	CH

Clive Hardy
Capt & Adjt.
for O/C cmdg,
2/12 Bn London Regt.

3cm
3009/10
96cm

WAR DIARY
OF
2/12th LONDON REGT

Vol 142

17/58

Army Form C. 2118.

WAR DIARY
or
INTELLIGENCE SUMMARY. 2/12 LONDON REGT (THE RANGERS)

(Erase heading not required.)

Instructions regarding War Diaries and Intelligence Summaries are contained in F.S. Regs., Part II. and the Staff Manual respectively. Title pages will be prepared in manuscript.

Page 1

Place	Date	Hour	Summary of Events and Information	Remarks and references to Appendices
LONGBRIDGE DEVERILL	Jan 4 1917	—	First day of Mobilisation.	R.R.S.
WARMINSTER	Feb 5th	8.20am	1st train load entrain consisting of 19 Officers, 484 N.C.Os & men, 32 horses, 10 vehicles 9 bicycles. Commanded by Col A.S. BARHAM V.D.	R.R.S.
"		9.20am	2nd train load entrain consisting of 18 Officers, 485 N.C.Os & men, 32 horses, 10 vehicles 1 bicycle. Commanded by Major S. CHART.	R.R.S.
SOUTHAMPTON		10.25am	1st train load detrained at SOUTHAMPTON	R.R.S.
"		11.30am	2nd train load detrained at SOUTHAMPTON.	R.R.S.
"		4.30pm	MAJOR CHART (in command) Lt SOLOMON, 2Lts WARREN and CUNNINGHAM, and 179 other ranks with all Bn transport embarked on board T. Ship MILLER	R.R.S.
"		5.30pm	Remainder of Bn embarked on board T.S. VIPER. Col A.S. BARHAM O.C. troops on board	R.R.S.
HAVRE	Feb 6	4.30am	Bn. on board T. Ship VIPER disembarked at HAVRE	R.R.S.
			Remainder of Bn. disembarked at same port later in the morning. On completing disembarkation both detachments of the Bn moved into No 1 Camp HAVRE	R.R.S. R.R.S.
"		Noon	Accommodation at this Camp very poor under canvas. Snow 4 to 6 ins on ground and temperature very low.	R.R.S.

Army Form C. 2118.

WAR DIARY
or
~~INTELLIGENCE~~ SUMMARY.

2/12 LONDON REGT. (THE RANGERS)

(Erase heading not required.)

Instructions regarding War Diaries and Intelligence Summaries are contained in F. S. Regs., Part II. and the Staff Manual respectively. Title pages will be prepared in manuscript.

Page 2

Place	Date 1917	Hour	Summary of Events and Information	Remarks and references to Appendices
HAVRE	Feb. 7th	8am	The Bn. (less 300 Officers and O.R.) entrained at the GARES DES MARCHANDISES HAVRE.	APPENDIX I. R.M.S
		10.30am	This train load moved out of HAVRE.	R.M.S
		9 pm	The remainder of the Bn entrained and moved out of HAVRE.	R.M.S
AUXI-LE-CHATEAUX.	Feb 8th	11.45 am	First train load of Bn detrained at AUXI-LE-CHATEAUX in the area of Concentration and marched to billets at WAVANS.	R.M.S
WAVANS	Feb 9th	9pm	2nd Party of Bn detrained at FRÉVANT and arrived at WAVANS billets at 3.30 am Feb 9th	R.M.S
	Feb 9th	—	Company arrangements.	R.M.S
	Feb 10th	—	Company arrangements	S.K.E
BEAUDRICOURT	Feb 11th	4.45 pm	Bn. (35 Officers 958 men) marched from billets at WAVANS to BEAUDRICOURT where Bn was accommodated in billets. Route WAVANS – GOUVIERES – Mon LE BLOND – BOUQUEMAISON	APPENDIX II R.M.S
			– L SOUICH – IVERGNY to BEAUDRICOURT.	
,,	Feb. 12	—	Company arrangements	R.M.S
,,	Feb 13	—	Company arrangements	R.M.S
,,	Feb 14	11.15am	The Bn. proceeded by motor lorries to LA CAUCHIE where platoons and HQrs were separated and joined Bns. of the 146th Infantry Bde who were holding the line in front of BAILLEULMONT. The Bn was attached to this Bde for instruction from	R.M.S

Army Form C. 2118.

WAR DIARY
or
INTELLIGENCE SUMMARY.
(Erase heading not required.)

Instructions regarding War Diaries and Intelligence Summaries are contained in F. S. Regs., Part II. and the Staff Manual respectively. Title pages will be prepared in manuscript.

Place	Date	Hour	Summary of Events and Information	Remarks and references to Appendices
	Feb 1917		Feb 14th to the 19th inclusive. One platoon to each Company of the Bde, and a guard of HqRangers HdQrs to each Bn HdQrs of the 146th Bde. There were no casualties in the Bn during this attachment.	R.W.S.
HALLOY	Feb 19	From 3.30 p.m	The Bn moved into billets at HALLOY by platoons at intervals. The billets were dirty and unhealthy.	R.W.S. APPENDIX IV
"	Feb 20		Company arrangements. Billets cleaned and village area cleaned up.	R.W.S.
"	Feb 21		Company arrangements.	R.W.S.
"	Feb 22	—	Company arrangements. Brigadier General H.C. JACKSON, D.S.O. Commanding 175th Inf BDE lectured to all officers of the Bn, chiefly on formation and the attack.	R.W.S.
"		5 p.m		
"	Feb 23	11 a.m.	Demonstration, near HURTEBISE FARM, for C.O.s, Company Commanders on the new attack formation and method of attack as laid down by G.H.Q. Pamphlet.	R.W.S.
"	Feb 24	Morning	All ranks had their box respirators tested in a gas atmosphere.	R.W.S.
"		2.30 p.m	Conference of Bn Commander and Adjutant at BDE H.Q. POMMERA. Taking over the sector of the line discussed.	R.W.S.
"	Feb 25	12.40 a.m	Message received that Bn was to be in readiness to move at short notice after	R.W.S.

T2134. Wt. W708—776. 500000. 4/15. Sir J. C. & S.

Army Form C. 2118.

WAR DIARY
or
INTELLIGENCE SUMMARY. 2/12 London Regt. (The Rangers)
(Erase heading not required.)

Place	Date	Hour	Summary of Events and Information	Remarks and references to Appendices
Page 3	4/3/1917			
HALLOY	Feb 25	5am	50am. Companies notified and were ready accordingly. The enemy had shown indication of having retired on V Corps front. Order to resume normal received.	R.W.S.
		8.15am	at 8.15 am	R.W.S.
		10.15am	Church Parade.	R.W.S.
	Feb 26	10.30am	The Bn less D Co practised the attack near HURTEBISE FARM.	R.W.S.
	Feb 27		Company arrangements. 50 men & Co. and Co. L. Gunners carry out L.G. practice. Three platoons at PAS assisting R.E.s 2nd Quarry Sy.	

28 Feb. 1917.

Arthur S Radcliffe. Col.
Comdg 2/12 London

Vol 3.

Confidential.

War Diary

of

2/12th Londons ("The Rangers")

From :- February 28th/1917 to March 26th/1917.

Volume 1.

WAR DIARY
INTELLIGENCE SUMMARY
(Erase heading not required.)

Army Form C. 2118.

2/12 LONDONS.

Page 4 Vol I

Place	Date	Hour	Summary of Events and Information	Remarks and references to Appendices
	Feb 1917			
HALLOY	28/2/17	8am	5 Officers and 16 platoons sent to PAS for assaulting R. E. in quarrying chalk, and wood cutting. Remainder of Bn practice trench assault and attend bathing parade at Divl. Baths at PAS during morning and afternoon.	RKS
	March 1/3/17	10am	A.C.Co practice trench assault in morning. Remainder of Bn of A & C Cos who have not fired with L.G. carry out L.G. practice.	RKS
HALLOY to BAILLEULVAL	2/3/17	8.30am	Bn marched to BAILLEULVAL. Roads between LAHERLIÈRE and BAILLEULVAL very much cut up due to heavy traffic after the thaw.	APPENDIX V RKS RKS
BAILLEULVAL	3/3/17		Company arrangements	RKS
BAILLEULVAL	4/3/17		C.O., Adjt, and Company Commanders made a reconnaissance of sector F2 to be taken over next day.	RKS
WAILLY	5/3/17	2.30pm	The Bn completed relief of 2/11th Bn in F2 sector. Co. disposed as follows C, D & A Cos from right to left in front line in that order. two platoons, B Co in reserve on reserve line and one platoon in each of WAILLY and PETIT CHATEAU KEEPS.(CMS) trenches & Bn. Hd. Qrs at The QUARRY.	RKS
	6/3/17		Situation normal.	RKS
	7/3/17		Situation normal. G.O.C. Division & G.O.C. Bde visited this sector and made a reconnaissance of SAP Z9a.	RKS

Army Form C. 2118.

WAR DIARY
or
INTELLIGENCE SUMMARY.
(Erase heading not required.)

2/12th LONDON REGT.

Place	Date	Hour	Summary of Events and Information	Remarks and references to Appendices
Page 5. Vol I. WAILY (Sect 3)	March 8th	10 a.m.	Companies completed their new dispositions in accordance with the new scheme of defence (SBM 616 the 4th). Under this scheme the subsector is defended as follows:— a. Two Companies on the frontage (normally held by three companies disposed as follows: Four platoons forming the Picquet and Groups line. Four platoons in the Support line in posts prepared for all round defence. b. Two platoons of another Company on the reserve line, and the other 2 platoons of this Company at WAILY and PETIT CHATEAU KEEPS respectively. c. The remaining company occupy hullets (chiefly cellars) in the village of WAILY, and are available as a Bn reserve. C and A Companies occupied the Picquet and Group line from right to left in that order. D Company furnished the garrison for the reserve line and both KEEPS. B Co. withdrew to the village of WAILY.	RWS
WAILY (Sector F2)	11th	11 a.m.	Companies of the Bn changed over positions B & D Co. took over strongpoints in the support line. A Co. came back to the reserve line and Keeps. C Co came back to WAILY and occupied not hullets there. Major CHART, 2 Lt & Adjt L.K. SPENCER, Lt de SAULLES, Lt AMSDEN came back to not Capt ELLIS	RWS

WAR DIARY
or
INTELLIGENCE SUMMARY.
(Erase heading not required.)

Army Form C. 2118.

2/12 LONDON REGT
(THE RANGERS)

Place	Date	Hour	Summary of Events and Information	Remarks and references to Appendices
Page 6 Vol I				
	March 12th 15		Billets at BELLACOURT for 4 days. 2 Lt CARTE arrived from Base as reinforcement.	RKS RKS
WAILLY (Sector F2)		6.20p	Companies changed over positions. A & C in Strong points, B in reserve line and Keeps. D Co in Bn billets at WAILLY. Col HOBRAHAM V.D, Lt WILLETT, 2Lt CLARKE, & 2Lt WARRENER went to meet at BELLACOURT section the C.O who new to Bde H.Q. at BRETENCOURT CHATEAU. MAJOR CHANT left in Finchley in command of Bn. First man of Bn killed by GERMAN Sniper whilst carrying message between Bn. HQrs and Bde HQrs.	RKS RKS RKS
	17th	5pm	Information received from 175" Inf Bde that enemy was falling back on VIIth Corps front which includes BAPAUME. Later in the day HQ Bde informed us that there were signs of the enemy retiring on our right as near as BUCQUOY GRABEN. At 7pm message was received from Bde that MONCHY appeared unoccupied. From observation on our front the enemy appeared to be preparing to retire. Range finders were seen in the direction of FICHEUX and BLAIRVILLE, together with many explosions at varying distances behind the German lines.	Appendix VI
	18th	2.50a	A report was received from 175 Bde that BOCHES had retired on the front of the 2 Bns immediately on our right (Sectors F1 and D) Patrols were sent out to our front and 2Lt FOUCAR (left company) with 6 O.R.	RKS RKS

Army Form C. 2118.

WAR DIARY
or
INTELLIGENCE SUMMARY.
(Erase heading not required.)

2/12 LONDON REGT
(THE RANGERS)

Instructions regarding War Diaries and Intelligence Summaries are contained in F. S. Regs., Part II. and the Staff Manual respectively. Title pages will be prepared in manuscript.

Place	Date	Hour	Summary of Events and Information	Remarks and references to Appendices
Page 4 Vol I	March		entered the GERMAN front line trenches and discovered that GERMANS had vacated them.	RKS
		6.30am	One Company (D) occupied German front line trench and about one hour 2 platoons of C and 2 platoons of A.C. reinforced D Co in occupation of GERMAN third line trench in rear of F₂ Sectn, and consolidated it. This line became our new front line with CAPT R.L. BURNSIDE in command of it {COL. BARNHAM and then BRUN from view, upon the B.N. at BELLACOURT}	APPENDIX VII
		6.30pm	D Co. were pushed forward for outpost duty with his left on the MADELEINE REDOUBT (M.27.a. Map 51GSW) in the second system of German trenches to M.32.c.6020 (Map 51GSW). A Bn of the KINGS LIVERPOOL REGT was on our left and 2/10 LONDONS on our right. No resistance was met with by D Co. on moving forward to this outpost line.	APPENDIX VIII RKS.
	19th	9.15am	Bn HQ. and each Co. has D Co. moved independently to and occupied FICHEUX. D Co was withdrawn from outpost line and reached FICHEUX late during the morning. FICHEUX was found to be literally laid to the ground; demolitions of all houses, wells, the cross roads, had been very thorough. On arrival at FICHEUX the Bn proceeded to make temporary shelters with whatever material was at hand, B Co furnished the outpost protection for the Bn. Other troops were now well in front of FICHEUX about BOYELLES in	APPENDIX IX RKS

T2134. Wt. W708/776. 500000. 4/15. Sir J. C. & S.

Army Form C. 2118.

WAR DIARY
or
INTELLIGENCE SUMMARY.
(Erase heading not required.)

2/12 LONDON REGT
THE RANGERS.

Instructions regarding War Diaries and Intelligence Summaries are contained in F. S. Regs., Part II. and the Staff Manual respectively. Title pages will be prepared in manuscript.

Place	Date	Hour	Summary of Events and Information	Remarks and references to Appendices
Page 8. Vol. I FICHEUX	March		Contact with small enemy patrols of the enemy.	R&S
			The following Officers and 31 men reported at Bn HdQrs as reinforcements sent up for base:- 2Lts WALLAEEF, T.C. WESTON, K.H.S. CLARKE, L.S. VOLTA. Drawn transport from XVIII to VII Corps.	R&S
	20th	10am	All Companies engaged on Salvage work in trenches F2 Sector.	R&S
		3pm	The Bn moved out of FICHEUX to billets at BRETENCOURT and GROSVILLE.	R&S
	21st	10am	The Bn employed on Salvage work in trenches F2 Sector.	R&S
	22nd	9.30am	The Bn moved out of BRETENCOURT and GROSVILLE and marched to billets at BAVINCOURT (A, B & D Cos) and LAHERLIERE (HdQrs & C Co).	R&S
	23.9.24th		Company arrangements for platoon training.	R&S
	25th	9.30am	Companies moved out of billets at BAVINCOURT and LAHERLIERE and proceeded independently to billets previously occupied at HALLOY.	R&S
	26th		Company arrangements for platoon training.	
			The supply of leather for repairs and also of new boots has been totally inadequate since landing in FRANCE. The leather supplied has been sufficient for 75 pairs of soles only. Indents put in on 8th Feb are still unsatisfied. There has consequently been a large number of sore feet. At this date there are 196 (25.1%) O.R. whose boots are in need of repair and 138 (17.7%) whose boots	R&S

Army Form C. 2118.

2/12 LONDON REGT
(THE RANGERS)

WAR DIARY
or
INTELLIGENCE SUMMARY.
(Erase heading not required.)

Instructions regarding War Diaries and Intelligence Summaries are contained in F. S. Regs., Part II. and the Staff Manual respectively. Title pages will be prepared in manuscript.

Place	Date	Hour	Summary of Events and Information	Remarks and references to Appendices
Page 9 Vol I			are past repair and need to be replaced. There 422.8 % are not effectively shod.	Oss
			Arthur S Mahon Col. Commanding 2/12th LONDONS	

T2134. Wt. W708—776. 500000. 4/15. Sir J. C. & S.

Vol 4 175/58

CONFIDENTIAL.

War Diary
of
2/12 London Regt
(The Rangers)

From March 27ᵗʰ To April 26ᵗʰ
1917.

Volume I

Army Form C. 2118.

WAR DIARY
or
INTELLIGENCE SUMMARY.
(Erase heading not required.)

2/12th LONDON REGT
(THE RANGERS)

Instructions regarding War Diaries and Intelligence Summaries are contained in F.S. Regs., Part II. and the Staff Manual respectively. Title pages will be prepared in manuscript.

Place	Date	Hour	Summary of Events and Information	Remarks and references to Appendices
Page 10 VOL 1				
HALLOY	27 March		Company arrangements for Platoon training. Rifle Grenade accident occurred whilst at Halloy. Platoon training and 2 O.R.s injured and the L. Inskilg Sergeant was killed.	P.L.S
	28th		Training exercise carried out by all companies consisting of intensive digging.	P.L.S
	29th		Field firing with rifle and L.G. CAPT H. SHEPHERD reported from 2/9 Lon Regt as Transport Officer.	P.L.S
	30th		Platoon training. HON LIEUT Q.M. F.J. PEARCE returned to ENGLAND, Lt SOLOMON took over duty as Q.M.	P.L.S
	31st		Platoon training, and L.G. practice. All Rifle Grenade Sections arrived in firing rifle grenades.	P.L.S
	April 1st	10.45 AM	The Bn moved out of HALLOY and marched into billets at NEUVILLETTE by the following route BEAUREPAIRE – DOULLENS – HAUTE VISÉE.	APPENDIX 11 P.L.S
NEUVILLETTE	2	10.15 am	The Bn marched from NEUVILLETTE to NOEUX by the following route – BARLY – REMAISNIL – FROHEN le GRAND – WAVANS. About BARLY the roads were steep in places and difficult for transport. At FROHEN le GRAND the roads were in great need of repair.	P.L.S P.L.S
	3		Special attention given by Companies to cleaning equipment and clothing.	P.L.S
NOEUX	5	9.30 am	The Bn moved out of billets at NOEUX and were taken by lorries and buses to BUS–les–ARTOIS where companies occupied huts at the South end of the village.	APPENDIX 12 P.L.S

Army Form C. 2118.

WAR DIARY
or
INTELLIGENCE SUMMARY.
(Erase heading not required.)

2/12 LONDON REGT.
(THE RANGERS)

Page 11 Vol I

Place	Date	Hour	Summary of Events and Information	Remarks and references to Appendices
Bus les Artois	April 6 (Good Friday)	10am & 10:45am	Two Companies at a time attended a church service at 10am & 10:45am respectively.	RUS
Miraumont	8	9am	The Bn moved by march route to MIRAUMONT	RUS APPENDIX 13
"	9		Four companies were employed on Railway Construction at ACHIET le GRAND	RUS
Achiet le Petit	10		The Bn less Head Quarters were employed on Railway Construction at ACHIET le GRAND and a Company of work moved into billets at ACHIET le PETIT.	RUS
"	12		Three Companies employed at ACHIET le GRAND and one Company at PUISIEUX employed on railway construction work.	RUS
"	13		Company arrangements for platoon training. Three hundred men employed on railway construction work. Remainder Pl-Company training.	RUS
"	14			
"	16		A + D Companies inspected by Company Officer in fighting order. Training in Bombers. Grenades and platoon training by all companies during the day.	RUS
"	17		The Bn employed on railway construction work on a new line being constructed between PUISIEUX and ACHIET le PETIT.	RUS
"	18		Training carried on under Co arrangements. Heavy rain all day.	RUS
"	19		Training carried under Bn arrangements.	RUS

Army Form C. 2118.

WAR DIARY
or
INTELLIGENCE SUMMARY.
(Erase heading not required.)

2/12 LONDONS.
(THE RANGERS)

Instructions regarding War Diaries and Intelligence Summaries are contained in F.S. Regs., Part II. and the Staff Manual respectively. Title pages will be prepared in manuscript.

Page 12
Vol I

Place	Date	Hour	Summary of Events and Information	Remarks and references to Appendices
ACHIET L. PETIT.	April 20th		The four companies were employed on railway construction work at the Light Railway which crosses the BAPAUME – ERVILLERS ROAD.	Ref
"	21st		Bde Training Exercise – The Bn in attack on a gun fortage. Normal formations adopted as had been and overcame strong points constructed during the consolidation of the position.	Ref
"	22nd		The Bn less HдQrs were employed on Railway construction at PUISIEUX and road construction at ACHIET L. GRAND.	Ref
"	23rd		B Co proceeded as the termination of work to ACHIET L. GRAND and were interposed near the station ready for unloading trains as they arrived.	Ref
"	24th		200 men employed on railway construction work at MIRAUMONT remainder of Bn except B Co carry out platoon training. Two Companies and one platoon employed at MIRAUMONT on railway construction and salvage work. B Co returned from ACHIET L. GRAND & billets previously occupied at ACHIET L. PETIT.	Ref
"	25th		Platoon training in accordance with Bde Programme.	Ref
"	26th	noon	GENERAL SIR H.H.de la P. GOUGH K.C.B. Commander of Fifth Army inspected	Ref

WAR DIARY
or
INTELLIGENCE SUMMARY.
(Erase heading not required.)

Army Form C. 2118.

Place	Date	Hour	Summary of Events and Information	Remarks and references to Appendices
Page 13	April			
AUBIGNY	26th		HQ Bde while on platoon training.	R.S
PETIT.		3pm	Bde. Exercise — outposts.	

Arthur Statham
Col. Commanding
2/12 London Regt.

C O N F I D E N T I A L.

W A R   D I A R Y

of

2/12th. BN. LDN. REGT.

(THE RANGERS).

From 27th. April 1917 to 27th. May 1917.

V O L U M E   4

Army Form C. 2118.

WAR DIARY
or
INTELLIGENCE SUMMARY.
(Erase heading not required.)

2/12 LONDON REGT.
(THE RANGERS)

Instructions regarding War Diaries and Intelligence Summaries are contained in F.S. Regs, Part II. and the Staff Manual respectively. Title pages will be prepared in manuscript.

Place	Date	Hour	Summary of Events and Information	Remarks and references to Appendices
Page 14 Vol I				
ACHIET le PETIT	April 27th	9.30am	Brig. Gen. H.S. Jackson. D.S.O. Commanding 175th Inf Bde inspected the Bn.	R&S
		2.30p	Brigade Exercise — Attack through LOGEAST WOOD.	R&S
	28th		Company arrangements. Officers Squad B. carried on a Regtl. Tour of Instruction under Major S. CHART.	R&S
		noon	Brig. Gen H.S. JACKSON D.S.O. inspected the billets occupied by this Bn.	R&S
	29th		Three Companies proceeded to ACHIET le GRAND for loading and unloading trucks. Two platoons went to Y Corps Musketry Officer employed on constructing a rifle range in ACHIET le PETIT.	R&S
			OFFICERS Courses in Physical Training and Bayonet Fighting, Lewis Gun, and Bombing were carried on under Bn arrangements. Signals and Snipers carried out Specialist training.	R&S
	30th		Three Companies proceeded to ACHIET le GRAND for loading and unloading railway trucks. Two platoons continued work on rifle range. Two platoons of B Co inspected by C.O and Major S. CHART. respectively. Squad A Officers taken over neighbourhood for instruction in tactics. Signals carried on Specialist training. 2 Lt E.R. BURTON reported as reinforcement posted to B Coy.	R&S R&S
	May 1st		Three Companies proceeded to ACHIET le GRAND for loading and unloading railway trucks. Two platoons continued work on rifle range. Officers Squad B. carried on a regimental tour in the morning and afternoon under Major CHART and the C.O respectively.	R&S
			Nos. 10 & 12 Plns. inspected, one in the morning one in the afternoon by the C.O. & Major S. CHART respectively.	R&S

WAR DIARY
INTELLIGENCE SUMMARY
(Erase heading not required.)

Army Form C. 2118.

2/12 LONDON REGT.
(THE RANGERS)

Place	Date	Hour	Summary of Events and Information	Remarks and references to Appendices
Page 15 Vol I	May 2nd		Company arrangements. No training entered after 10 am. Officers courses on Physical Training, Bayonet fighting and Lewis Gun were held.	Q & S
	" 3rd		BCompany employed on Salvage and clearing work at PARAMOUNT, two platoons of C Coy were employed on the Rifle Range ACHIET le PETIT and 1 platoon of C were employed in the village of ACHIET le PETIT. Remainder were training under Coy. arrangements including range practice.	Q & S
	" 4th	1.30 pm	The Bn marched with the Bde to a position ¾ mile South of LAGNICOURT, and relieved the 8th AUSTRALIAN I.F. who were in support to 6th AUSTRALIAN I.F. All ranks occupied shelters made by small excavations on the East side of a sunken road covered with tarpaulins. Relief completed by 11 pm.	Q & S
	" 5th	9.30 pm	The Bn relieved the 4th AUSTRALIAN I.F. who occupied the left section of the Bde Sector. The front extended from C 18 b to C 12 a and consisted of a line of picquet posts with supports, with two Coys 2 platoons in Bn reserve along the LAGNICOURT – NOREUIL Road. The position faced QUÉANT. Bn H/Qrs was at C 17 d 90 in a sunken road.	Q & S
	6th		On the night of 4/5 May 2 Lt S E MUNN and 3 N.C.O.Rs were slightly wounded	

WAR DIARY
INTELLIGENCE SUMMARY

2/12 LONDON REGT. (The Rangers)

Army Form C. 2118.

Place	Date	Hour	Summary of Events and Information	Remarks and references to Appendices
Page/6 Vol 1.	May 9th		and two O.Rs were missing, as the result of an encounter between a patrol of C Coy under 2Lt Munn and a German patrol near the Sunken road about C12 b 9.8. 2Lt Munn returned to duty next day. Two O.Rs & 1 N.C.O were wounded whilst filling in Shell holes	R.W.D
			1 NCO and 3 men were wounded whilst laying German heavy Gun ammn dead in rear of Piquet line.	
		9.30 p	The 2/10th Bn relieved this Bn. The relief was completed about 1 am. May 10. The Bn took over the left support position of the Bde sector which was occupied by RANGERS on the night 4th–5th May. Two O.Rs & 9 B Co were wounded just before the relay took place on the march up to this subsector both on our and hostile artillery	R.W.D
			During the four days in this subsector both our and hostile artillery were very active but very few casualties were sustained — total 11 O.Rs.	
K.	11th	9.30 p	The Bn were relieved by the 30th Aust. Inf. Regt. Two Cos remained and were employed until 2 am on wiring, on completion of which they rejoined the Bn at the BEUGNY – YTRES line South of VAULX	R.W.D
	12th	6 pm	The Bn moved by platoons to a standing camp on the west side of the village of FAVREUIL.	B.S.
	14th		Co arrangements and Bn Drill. Training by platoons in rifle patrols etc.	R.W.D
	15	3 pm	Bn moved by platoons to standing camp near BIHUCOURT.	R.W.D

Army Form C. 2118.

WAR DIARY
or
INTELLIGENCE SUMMARY. 2/12 LONDON REGT. THE RANGERS
(Erase heading not required.)

Instructions regarding War Diaries and Intelligence Summaries are contained in F.S. Regs., Part II and the Staff Manual respectively. Title pages will be prepared in manuscript.

Page 17 Vol 1.

Place	Date	Hour	Summary of Events and Information	Remarks and references to Appendices
BIHUCOURT	May 16 1917		Company arrangements for training. The Bn with remainder of Bde were subjected to a cloud gas for men.	R&S O&S
	19"		The Bn moved into support position of the Bde Sector (from U.29 A.6.0 to U.22 c.0.3) relieving 2/3rd LONDONS. about Cos were disposed as follows relieving Cos of the 2/3 LONDONS. HQ and C Co. on Rly Embankment about C.3.a.3.4. B & A Co (from Right Half) in trench from U.29 c.7.3 to U.28 d.3.8. D Co in trench C.10.b.9.1 to C.10.a.0.4. During the occupation of this position Cos sectors was intermittently shelled. Cos were without dug outs except the Co. on Rly Embankment and the trenches occupied by A, B & D Co were badly constructed affording little cover and no comfort. Communication by day could be observed and traffic was reduced to a minimum. Supplies including water in petrol tins were carried from a dump 800 yds in rear of D.C. Carrying parties were supplied by 2/1 Bn holding the front line, to carry up supplies of food water and R.E material, which each nly be carried up to Loos line by night.	BULLECOURT APPENDIX 14 R&S

WAR DIARY
or
INTELLIGENCE SUMMARY.
(Erase heading not required.)

Army Form C. 2118.

2/12 LONDON REGT (THE RANGERS)

Place	Date	Hour	Summary of Events and Information	Remarks and references to Appendices
Page 16 Vol 1.				
	20th		During the four days occupation of the support position the Bn sustained casualties as follows:-	
	21st		6 O.R. wounded.	RWS
	22nd		10 O.R. wounded.	
	23rd		2Lt. J.C WESTON and 6 O.R. wounded	RWS
			2Lt. F. LACEY and 20 O.R wounded, 2Lt VOLTA and 2 O.R. shell shock.	Appendix 15
	23/24		The Bn relieved 2/11 Bn on night of 23/24th May, in the four line of this Brigade on the right of Bullecourt. An Australian Bn was on our right flank and the 2/9 Londons were on our left in four of Bullecourt. (The Bn frontage had been extended to a two Bn frontage.) Cos were disposed as follows D.C.B.A. from right to left each with two platoons in the four line and two in the support line. Battalion four frontage of about 1000 yds was divided into two sub sectors each of two Companies, the right sub sector commanded by Col. A.S. BARHAM the left sub sector by MAJOR S. CHART, each with their head quarters on the return flanks of the support line.	RWS RWS

Army Form C. 2118.

WAR DIARY
or
INTELLIGENCE SUMMARY.

1/12 LONDON REGT.
(THE RANGERS)

(Erase heading not required.)

Page 19
Vol. 1.

Place	Date	Hour	Summary of Events and Information	Remarks and references to Appendices
			The conditions in the trenches were very bad. A very large number of unburied dead were scattered in and near the trenches, while a large number were lightly buried in the parapets or in the trenches themselves. The trenches and ground near them had been continuously and heavily shelled; in places the parapets were blown away making movement in the trenches to be avoided, and from the first by the enemy. Work was begun immediately to deepen the existing trenches, bury the dead, and salve rifles & equipment in the area by men of the firing line. Movement during the day was reduced to a minimum and most of the work was carried on during the night. During the day the enemy's artillery and snipers were very active, and accurate. The casualties in the Bn were as follows :-	
	May 24th		4 killed i/c F.T. HILLS and 25 other ranks wounded.	R&S
	25th		3 O.Rs wounded	R&S
	26th		3 O.Rs killed 5 O.Rs wounded and 2 suffering from shell shock.	R&S
	27th		5 O.Rs killed 8 O.Rs wounded.	R&S
				R&S

T2134. Wt. W708—776. 500000. 4/15. Sir J. C. & S.

Army Form C. 2118.

WAR DIARY
or
INTELLIGENCE SUMMARY.
(Erase heading not required.)

2/12 LONDON REGT
(THE RANGERS).

Page 20.
Vol. 1.

Date	Hour	Summary of Events and Information	Remarks and references to Appendices
May 24/25		On night of May 24th, 25th dispositions of Coy. were re-arranged as follows:- C Co was brought back to the trench from U.29.c.7.3. to U.28.d.3.8., and one platoon front of D & B Co. was pushed forward to the from line overlapping the position of the two front platoons of C.C.; Bn Hd Qrs. moved back to the Rly Embankment.	APPENDIX 16. Q & S
26/27		The Bn was relieved by 2/8 Londons, and marched back by platoons as they were relieved, to the transport lines about B.30.a. Improved huts were ready & made use of by all ranks.	Q & S
27	6p	The Bn moved to a standing camp a mile distant about B.29.a. Col. A. S. BARHAM arrived in 10 days leave and MAJOR S. CHART assumed Command of the Bn.	Q & S

28/5/17.

Stephen Chart
Major.
Cmdg 2/12 Londons.

CONFIDENTIAL

War Diary
of
2/12 Londons (The Rangers)

from May 30th to June 30th 1917

Vol 5

WAR DIARY
INTELLIGENCE SUMMARY

Army Form C. 2118.

2/12 LONDONS (THE RANGERS)

Page 21 Vol I

Place	Date	Hour	Summary of Events and Information	Remarks and references to Appendices
	May 28		Company arrangements for platoon training, Lewis Gun & Signalling Courses were commenced in the Bn.	PMS
	June 3/4		The Bn proceeded to the support position and relieved the 2/8 Londons. Coy were disposed as follows A & B Cos occupied the NORIEUL – LONGATTE road, C Co. occupied the Rly Embankment and D. Co. occupied a Sunken road at C4 & 9 c. Bn H.Qrs was at ECOUST. While in this position the Bn was employed in joining the entrances in front of C Co position, and in deepening BULLECOURT AVENUE.	PMS APPENDIX 17 PMS PMS
	June 11"		The Bn moved forward and relieved the 2/x 1 LONDONS in the Right Bn. portion of the Bde front. The Bn front extended from U22c9730 on the right to U23c80.10 on the left. Bn H.Qrs were situated at U 28c 97.15. 2Lt WESTON J.C. of 16th LONDON REGT attached 2/pLondons died of wounds in hospital from wound in hostilities.	PMS PMS
	Night 19/20		The Bn held this part of the line for 4 days during which time our patrols and snipers were particularly successful. A German patrol of 9 men were seen approaching our lines, and after being challenged by our sentry was fired on. Two men were seen to fall	PMS

WAR DIARY or INTELLIGENCE SUMMARY

Army Form C. 2118.

2/12 LONDON REGT.
(THE RANGERS)

Page 22 Vol I.

Place	Date	Hour	Summary of Events and Information	Remarks and references to Appendices
Nyl	9/10 Jun 10th		and on examination later one was found to be a N.C.O. and the other a musketeer of the 180th R.I.R. On the evening of the 10th June a prisoner of the 180th R.I.R. was captured though in unwounded. Later that night a German officer of the 119th R.I.R. approached our lines having lost his way. He was challenged and shot by one of the 2/Rangers sentries, and afterwards brought into the Bn lines. Col A.S. BARHAM returned and resumed command of the Bn. 2Lt A.S. CARTE died of wounds in hospital.	CWS RWS
Nyl	10/11 Jun		Two prisoners both of the 119th R.I.R. were brought in unwounded. These men gave useful information of the German line immediately opposite the front of this Bn. During the occupation of this position by 2/Rangers the enemy was active and alert. His artillery shelled the front and support line of the Bn intermittently, but the sniping on the enemy's part was considerably reduced owing to the Bn's ascendancy in this direction	CWS RWS

Army Form C. 2118.

WAR DIARY
or
INTELLIGENCE SUMMARY.
(Erase heading not required.)

2/12 LONDONS
(THE RANGERS)

Place	Date	Hour	Summary of Events and Information	Remarks and references to Appendices
Page 23 (Vol 1)			A great deal of work was done in the trenches but for the defence and comfort of the line.	Cus
			The total casualties sustained were 2 Lt CARTE died of wounds, 13 O.R. killed and 2 Lt. Munro & 39 O.Rs wounded.	Rus
	Night 14/15 June		The Bn was relieved by 9th DEVON REGT, and marched back to a Stanley Camp near MORY	APPENDIX 18 Rus
			During the next 3 days the Bn carried on Platoon training. The attack was practised on a taped out position by platoons, by Co, by the Bn	
	19th		and on the 19th June in conjunction with the 2/9th LONDONS.	Rus
	20	9am	The C.O inspected A Co in full work.	Rus
		11am	The G.O.C. 175 Inf Bde inspected the Bn Transport animals	
	Night 20/21		The Bn proceeded to 174 Bde Sector N.W. of BULLECOURT and commenced to dig a C.T. running back from the new captured front line (which was the "HINDENBURG FRONT line) at U.20.a. 8.9 accross TIGER Trench to U.19. b.8.5. The Bn returned to MORY Camp about 4 am.	Rus
	Night 22/23		The C.T. commenced on night of 20/21 June was completed by this Bn	Rus

Army Form C. 2118.

2/12 LONDON REGT
(THE RANGERS)

WAR DIARY
or
INTELLIGENCE SUMMARY.
(Erase heading not required.)

Place	Date	Hour	Summary of Events and Information	Remarks and references to Appendices
Page 24 Vol 1.				
"MORY"	June 24th	2pm	The 2/R.WARWICK REGT relieved this Bn or Mory Camp in Divisional Reserve.	APPENDIX 19 RWS
	25th		The Bn marched back to a camp in the South side of LOGEAST WOOD	RWS
			An instructive field firing competition was carried out under Bn arrangements.	

Arthur Strahan
Col.
Cmdg 2/12 LONDONS

30/6/17

Vol 7

CONFIDENTIAL

WAR DIARY
of
2/12th LONDON REGT.
(The Rangers)

FROM — June 25th. 1917
TO — July 31st. 1917

VOL. VI

Army Form C. 2118.

WAR DIARY
or
INTELLIGENCE SUMMARY.   2/12 LONDONS.
(Erase heading not required.)   (THE RANGERS).

Instructions regarding War Diaries and Intelligence Summaries are contained in F.S. Regs., Part II. and the Staff Manual respectively. Title pages will be prepared in manuscript.

Place	Date	Hour	Summary of Events and Information	Remarks and references to Appendices
LOGEAST WOOD	June 25th July 1st	5. Manning.		
	July 2nd	11a.m	G.O.C. 58th Div. inspected the Bde.	
	3rd		The Bn. moved by Rattrack with the Bde. to BAPAUME.	APPENDIX XII
	5th		Moved to BERTINCOURT. Transport proceeded independently to YTRES. (Bn. Transport lines)	RWS
	6th		Night of 7/8th. Moved by light Railway to HAVRINCOURT WOOD and took over the left	
	8th		Bn. Rd. Sector with the trench line relieving the 1/5" MANCHESTER REGT.	RWS
HAVRINCOURT WOOD			The Battalion consisted of three main lines – the "Outpost," "Front" and Reserve".	RWS
			D.C. & A Cos. from right to left in Rear were held the outpost, and four his each	
			with platoons in each line – B Co. held the Reserve line. The Right n. Coy.	
			boundary was at K.33.C.9.0. – The left n. West boundary was on the Canal	
			Du NORD (K.26.C.7.0.) Bn. Hd. Qrs. was at Q.2.C.R.6.	
			The GERMAN and our Front lines were a spirited slow of a valley, – our	RWS
			left flank Company holding a large chalk heap, known as YORKSHIRE	
			BANK, which was a conspicuous landmark on the East bank of the duty.	
			du Canal	RWS
			There was little artillery activity and the GERMAN Infy were apparently	

Army Form C. 2118.

WAR DIARY
or
INTELLIGENCE SUMMARY.

2/12 LONDONS
(THE RANGERS)

(Erase heading not required.)

Place	Date	Hour	Summary of Events and Information	Remarks and references to Appendices
Page 26 Vol 1.				
HAVRINCOURT WOOD			very inactive during the day — Seen was of movement in the GERMAN line was extremely rare during any day. During the night however the GERMAN garrison pushed out listening posts, and machine gun posts. Patrolling on both sides during darkness was active, and patrols of the enemy were frequently in contact with our own. Trench mortars were used by the enemy against both our flanks. On the night of 11/12 July in accordance with orders received 2Lt C.H.A. GALBRAITH and 20 other ranks forming a strong fighting patrol attempted to reconnoitre DEAN COPSE and to ascertain the nature of an artillery bombardment. The patrol came under heavy M.G. rifle fire from flanks and eventually withdrew still their casualties amounted by the Bn were while holding this part of the line the Casualties sustained by the Bn were 2Lt A.J. WARREN (Att. 10th) and 3 other ranks killed; 2Lt C.H.A. GALBRAITH and 8 other ranks wounded.	R.W.S R.W.S R.W.S
	July 16/17.		On the night of 14/7 July the Bn was relieved by the 2/11 LONDONS and moved to the Bde Reserve position. Bn Hd Qrs KDIE.O.O.	APPENDIX X/X Reg

T2134. Wt. W708-776. 500000. 4/15. Sir J. C. & S.

Army Form C. 2118.

WAR DIARY
or
INTELLIGENCE SUMMARY.
(Erase heading not required.)

2/12 LONDON REGT
(THE RANGERS)

Page 27 Vol. 1.

Place	Date	Hour	Summary of Events and Information	Remarks and references to Appendices
			During the time of duty in the Bde Reserve Position the Bn furnished working parties, chiefly during the night. They were employed mainly on improving the outpost line and front line.	RWS
	Aug 20/21		The enemy attempted to raid the outpost line held by the 2/10th London. The raiders were driven off, but the Bn had 2 Co's were moved up to PLACE MONTMARE and Kance to 2/10 LONDONS HdQrs as a precautionary measure. Two Co's were already near the point where the raid took place engaged in working parties and assisted in the defence of the position. (closed)	APPENDIX XXI / XXII
	Aug 22		Between 10 am and 4 pm the Bn were relieved by the 2/9th LONDONS and moved back to billets at RUYAULCOURT in Divisional Reserve.	RWS
Nyshu9	23/24		2Lt ECV FOUCAR and 40 other ranks carried out a raid on WIGAN COPSE. Details of the raid and report are attached as appendices.	RWS APPENDIX XXIII
RUYAULCOURT	25-26		Bn in Reserve in Divisional Reserve by the 10th ARGYLL + SUTHERLAND HIGHLANDERS and marched to BERTINCOURT.	RWS
BERTINCOURT	27		March Buses, a Light Railway to BAPAUME where Bn entrained. Transport detrained at SAULTY locality a small portion which marched to DAINEVILLE in two stages.	APPENDIX XXIV / XX / FP17 RWS

T:134. Wt. W708—776. 500000. 4/15. Sir J.C.&S.

Army Form C. 2118.

WAR DIARY
or
INTELLIGENCE SUMMARY.
(Erase heading not required.)

2/12 LONDON REGT
(THE RANGERS)

Instructions regarding War Diaries and Intelligence Summaries are contained in F. S. Regs., Part II. and the Staff Manual respectively. Title pages will be prepared in manuscript.

Place	Date	Hour	Summary of Events and Information	Remarks and references to Appendices
Page 28 Vol 1.				
DAINEVILLE	27/7/17	11p	The Bn (less Transport) detrained at BEAUMETZ and marched to billets at DAINEVILLE — 2½ miles west of ARRAS.	Oh/S
	July 28 – 31st		Training.	
	31/7/17			

Arthur H Parker
Col. Comdg.
2/12 London.

Confidential

Vol 8

C O N F I D E N T I A L.
===========================

W A R   D I A R Y

of

2/12th. LONDONS (The Rangers)

------------------oOo------------------

From AUGUST 1st.   to   AUGUST 31st. 1917.

VOL. 1.
======

R.C.Spencer
Capt. & Adjt.,
for Col.,
Comdng. 2/12th. Bn. Ldn. Regt.

WAR DIARY or INTELLIGENCE SUMMARY.

2/12 LONDON REGT.
2/ RANGERS.

Army Form C. 2118.

(Erase heading not required.)

Page 20
Vol I

Place	Date	Hour	Summary of Events and Information	Remarks and references to Appendices
DAINVILLE	Aug 1st to 10th	Aug 11	Training.	PWS
	11th	4:30p	Bn less transport moved to WAGNONLIEU.	PWS
	13 to 17th	18	Training	PWS
	18th	2:30p	Moved to hutted Camp on South side of DUISANS	PWS
	19 to 23rd	24	Training.	PWS
Nyl or B	24/25th		Bn moved by train form ARRAS to PROVEN (new Bde. Railhead) Strength of Bn actually with unit 38 Officers 908 other ranks.	PWS APPENDIX XXV
	25th		Bn marched to BRAKE CAMP. 3 miles WNW of POPERINGHE	PWS
	26-28th		Training	PWS
	29th	9.30am	Moved to BROWN CAMP. 2 miles N.W. of POPERINGHE between CANAL de POPERINGHE and the POPERINGHE - ELVERDINGHE Road.	PWS
			Battle surplus personnel consisting of 6 officers 53 O.Rs proceeded to Bde. Depôt Bn at HOUTKERQUE	PWS
	30th	9.10a	Bn moved to DAMBRE CAMP.	PWS
	31st		Training.	PWS
				O

Arthur Maclean
Col Comdg
2/12 London

WAR DIARY or INTELLIGENCE SUMMARY

(Erase heading not required.)

Army Form C. 2118.

2/12 LONDONS
(THE RANGERS)

175 / 58

Place	Date	Hour	Summary of Events and Information	Remarks and references to Appendices
Page 30 Vol I. 1917	September 1st–5th		Training about DAMBRE CAMP.	
Ypres	6th		Bn relieved 2/XI Bn at CANAL BANK.	
	Night 9/10		Bn relieved 2/9th Bn in front of ST JULIEN. Bn Hd Qrs at HACKNEY VILLA. Casualties 14 O.R. killed 70 O.R. wounded.	
	Night 12/13th		Returned to CANAL BANK, being relieved at ST JULIEN by 2/1st LONDONS.	
Ypres Canal	13th		Bn moved back to BRAKE CAMP. Training.	
	14–19th		Training.	
	20.	11 am	Moved to REIGESBURG CAMP in DIVISIONAL RESERVE.	
	21st	7–10 pm	Relieved 2/XI Bn and Coy of 173rd Bde about ST JULIEN and CALIFORNIA DRIVE. Bn Hd Qrs at CHEDDAR VILLA.	
	22nd	8–10 pm	Relieved by 2/3rd LONDONS and moved back to CANAL BANK.	
	25th		Bn moved up to assembly position preparatory to attack on the ridge N.E. of ST JULIEN about AVIATIK Fm. BOETLEER – NILE.	APPENDIX XXVI
	26th	5.50 am	Zero hour for the attack. The Bn reached and held its objective, capturing about 60 unwounded prisoners and about 14 wounded prisoners. New Bn position were heavily attacked and shelled heavily during the afternoon but Boche did not gain a footing West of position gained by Bn. Total casualties were 2 Lts A.J.G. ROSE, B.K. HOOPER and W.K. GRIFFITH	

Army Form C. 2118.

WAR DIARY
or
INTELLIGENCE SUMMARY.
(Erase heading not required.)

2/12 LONDONS
(The RANGERS)

Place	Date	Hour	Summary of Events and Information	Remarks and references to Appendices
Page 31 Vol 1.	Sept.		killed. Capt F. WALLER, Capt C. HARDY, and 2Lt K H S CLARE wounded (the two latter remained at duty) 19 O.R. killed, 90 O.R. wounded and 6 O.R. missing.	
	27"		Several Counter attacks were attempted against our position but were driven of by Artillery, M.G, L.G & Rifle fire before they became serious.	
	27/28.	Night of 27/28.	Bn was relieved by 5 GLOUCESTERS and marched back to REISEBURG CAMP.	
	28"	3p	Bn moved to DAMBRE CAMP. Reinforced by 120 O.R. from Base.	
	29"		Bn rested.	
	30"		Moved to BRAKE CAMP.	

30/9/'17.

Stephen Chant
Major
Commdg. 2/12 Londons.

Vol 10

Confidential

War Diary Volume I.

2/12 2/12 Bn. London Regt.

October 1917.

Army Form C. 2118.

WAR DIARY
or
INTELLIGENCE SUMMARY.
(Erase heading not required.)

2/12 LONDON REGT
(THE RANGERS)

Instructions regarding War Diaries and Intelligence Summaries are contained in F.S. Regs., Part II. and the Staff Manual respectively. Title pages will be prepared in manuscript.

Place	Date	Hour	Summary of Events and Information	Remarks and references to Appendices
Page 32 Vol. 1.	October 1.		Bn entrained at VLAMERTINGHE and moved to AUDRUICQ. STN. thence to Billets about ZUTKERQUE.	RMS
	4th 8th		200 Officers, NCOs & men were taken to CALAIS by Busses. to spend a day at Seaside. 2 Officers and 60 other ranks were sent to Rest Camp at BOULOGNE for 14 days.	RMS
ZUTKERQUE	1-20		Training	
	21st		Bn entrained at AUDRUICQ STN and taken by train to HOPOUTRE STN, 2 KILOMETRES West from POPERINGHE. Bn marched to ROAD CAMP at SAN-TAN-TER-BIEZEN about 3 miles West of POPERINGHE.	RMS
	21st to 29th		Training.	
	30th		Bn moved by rail from RAILHOEK to REIGERSBURG thence by route march to huts at KEMPTON PARK about 3½ miles NE of YPRES.	RMS
	(24th		(settle nucleus detached from Bn to HOUTKERQUE)	

Arthur S Rankens
Col. Comdg.
2/12 London R.

Vol II

War Diary of
2/12 "
London Regiment
("The Rangers")
—
November
1917

Army Form C. 2118.

WAR DIARY
or
INTELLIGENCE SUMMARY.
(Erase heading not required.)

2/12 LONDON REGT
THE RANGERS.

Place	Date	Hour	Summary of Events and Information	Remarks and references to Appendices
KEMPTON PARK N.W. of YPRES.	Oct 31st		A Coy marched from KEMPTON Pk and occupied R. Bde Supt in position at PASH ANT TRENCH	
	Nov 1st		Bn (less A.Coy) were accommodated in huts at KEMPTON PARK in Bde Reserve.	
	2/5		Relieved 2/9 London in the Bn Outpost line in front of POELCAPPELLE. The ground was shattered, swampy and muddy. Marches also very protracted owing to darkness. Relief was commenced at dusk (about 5 p.m.) and was not completed until midnight. Coys were disposed as follows: B. at C Coys Rel A Fm relieving Bn frontage. The right flank extended to LEKKERBOTERBEEK – the left flank of the Bn was at REQUETE FM. D Coy was in support in the Pillboxes above the BREWERY (POELCAPPELLE) and 1/6 the Coy about GLOSTER FM.	
			Bn HdQrs were in a concrete pillbox at South end of POELCAPPELLE.	
VLAM.	Nov 4/5		Relieved by 2/4 x 1 London reserve the Bn which were marched to and occupied huts at CANAL BANK, near ESSEX FM.	
	6.		Bn marched to DRAKE CAMP and weapon huts transport now good & Bn from SIEGE CAMP	
	6-14		Training.	
	14th		Bn marched to FENTON CAMP Ridouts NE of PROVEN. Quarters consisted of tents and 70 men in barns. A Coy were detached in barns. Camp was in a very muddy condition.	

Army Form C. 2118.

WAR DIARY
or
INTELLIGENCE SUMMARY.
(Erase heading not required.)

Place	Date	Hour	Summary of Events and Information	Remarks and references to Appendices
PROVEN.	Nov. 15 & 16.		Training.	
	Nov. 17.		The Bn. marched to PARROY FARM about 1½ km E.S.E. of ELVERDINGHE and occupied shooners & dugouts. A Coy 2/4th Bn. was attached for work under orders of C.O. 2/12th Bn. Col. A.S. BARHAM relinquished the command of the Bn. & proceeded to England.	
	Nov. 18-24 incl.		Worked for 173rd & 183rd Coy. R.E. on Road making and mending principally near LANGEMARCK. Working Parties 5 - 600 men daily. Casualties O.R. 5 killed. 2 wounded.	
	Nov. 25.		Returned by train to PROVEN & occupied PENTON CAMP. Transport returned by road.	
	26.		Transport left by road for new area. Billeted at ST. MOMELIN for night.	
	27.		Moved by train to New Area - detrained at WIZERNES STATION marches to billets arriving about 11 p.m. Distribution. H.Q. & B. Coys. Q.M. Stores & Transport at SENINGHEM. A. C. & D. Coys. AFFRINGUES. Billets generally good & clean.	
	28 29 30		Rest - Cleaning Up & Refitting.	

Victor M Burnside
Capt & Adj
2/12th The Queen's Regt

Army Form C. 2118.

Page 35
Vol 1.

Instructions regarding War Diaries and Intelligence Summaries are contained in F.S. Regs., Part II. and the Staff Manual respectively. Title pages will be prepared in manuscript.

WAR DIARY
or
INTELLIGENCE SUMMARY.
(Erase heading not required.)

2/12 LONDON REGT
(The Rangers)

10/12

Place	Date	Hour	Summary of Events and Information	Remarks and references to Appendices
SENINGHEM & AFFRINGUES	Dec. 1 & 2.		Training.	
	3.		Bn. fired Classification Practices on Rifle Range VAL de LUMBRES.	
	4 & 5.		Training. Transport left by road on 5th for SIEGE CAMP. 1st Stage to ST. MOMELIN. 2nd Stage to ST JAN TER BIEZEN on 6th inst. Third Stage to SIEGE CAMP on 7th December	
	6.		The Bn. marched to LUMBRES and there entrained. They detrained at WIZERNES and entrained at the station at that place. They proceeded by train to ESSER DINGHE station and then marched to quarters at SIEGE CAMP. The Bn. was split up in four different camps.	
	7.		Resting and fitting for tour in the line.	
	8.		The Bn. took over the line from the 4th North Staffordshire Regt. Dispositions were as follows:- Front Line: B. Coy. at SOURD FARM & BANFF HOUSES – C. Coy. on left at SHAFT a neighbouring post. Coy HQ of both front coys. at BURNS HOUSE. Capt. L.B. BELL was in command of front line. Support Coy – B. Coy – two platoons near BURNS HOUSE and two platoons with Coy H.Q. at WINCHESTER FARM. Bn. H.Q. at ALBERTA. A. Coy. at CANAL BANK employed on various guards and working parties.	
	9.		In the line. Town was quiet.	
	10.		Relieved by 2nd INNISKILLIN FUSILIERS. Bn. marched back and occupied quarters at CANAL BANK. The relief commenced at 8 p.m. and was completed about midnight. The incoming Bn. established their HQ at HUBNER FARM.	
	11 & 12.		Resting and Refitting.	
	12/13.		On night 12/13th. The Bn. relieved the 2/8th Bn. London Regt. in the Brigade Outpost Line in and in front of POELCAPPELLE. The Bn. marched to KEMPTON PARK and after	

PAGE 36

WAR DIARY
or
INTELLIGENCE SUMMARY.
(Erase heading not required.)

Army Form C. 2118.

Place	Date	Hour	Summary of Events and Information	Remarks and references to Appendices
POELCAPPELLE	12/13		Bn. proceeded to the line. The Bn. were in Right Sub-Sector of Brigade front and were distributed as follows: B. Coy at TRAERS FARM & MEUSS and GLOSTER FARM with Coy H.Q. at GLOSTER. A Coy in POELCAPPELLE - SPRIET ROAD & MEUNIER and D. Coy at NOBLES - HELLES and POELCAPPELLE - with H.Q. at Brewery. Bn. H.Q. at NORFOLK HOUSE. C. Coy on Cornlee. Attack Coy at PHEASANT TRENCH.	
	13-14		The tour generally was quiet. Going was bad and visibility poor	
	14/15		The Bn. was relieved by 29th Bn. Relief was completed 10.30 p.m. C. Coy remained at PHEASANT TRENCH. The Bn remainder returned to KEMPTON PARK into Nisen - Support Bn.	
	15		Refitting	
	16		Relieved by 2/2nd Bn London Regt and returned by train - light-railway to DAWSON'S CORNER. Thence marched to WHITE MILL CAMP, ELVERDINGHE. Camp consisted of Nissen huts in good condition.	
	17-24		Refitting - Training - Inspections.	
	24/25		The Bn. moved by train to KEMPTON PARK. Thence marched to line relieving 2/2nd Bn London Regt. Relief was completed by 8.30 p.m. Dispositions - Bn. right - A in centre - Coy left. Bn. in the line. Ground was very hard. Weather frosty. Visibility at hand mainly good. Several nights were exceptionally light. Enemy Artillery was active on POELCAPPELLE throughout the tour. Progress was made in erecting wire round the various Melns and also in erecting Sandbag positions. Considerable E.A activity met by Lewis Guns. Anti-Aircraft fire. Support Coy worked under R.E's in making dugouts in PHEASANT TRENCH.	
	25-28			

Page 37 Vol 1.

Army Form C. 2118.

WAR DIARY
or
INTELLIGENCE SUMMARY.
(Erase heading not required.)

Place	Date	Hour	Summary of Events and Information	Remarks and references to Appendices
Poelcappelle.	28.		Bn. was relieved in Outpost line by 2/19th. Relief completed 9.30 p.m. B Coy joined D Coy in PHEASANT TRENCH under Batt. Precaution Order. Remainder at KEMPTON PARK. Right-Support Battn.	
	29-31		In Support. Two companies at KEMPTON PARK cleaning up and refitting. On night 31.12.17. Carrying parties of 40 + 25 regt. were sent by rear companies to outpost line.	

Clive Hardy
Major
Cmdg 9/Bn London Regt.

9 Infantry

War Diary

12th B (late 2/12 t) Bn Lond on Regt

From January 1st 1918
To January 31st 1918

Volume I

Page 1

Army Form C. 2118.

WAR DIARY
or
INTELLIGENCE SUMMARY.
(Erase heading not required.)

2/12 LONDON REGT.

Instructions regarding War Diaries and Intelligence Summaries are contained in F.S. Regs, Part II. and the Staff Manual respectively. Title pages will be prepared in manuscript.

Place	Date	Hour	Summary of Events and Information	Remarks and references to Appendices
	1918			
KEMPTON PK.	Jan 1.		Battn was relieved in Support by 2/2nd Londons & returned to WHITE MILL CAMP, ELVERDINGHE. The Bn moved by train from Battle to DAWSONS CORNER and reoccupied same billets as previously.	
	Jan 2-4.		Refitting, Training	
	Jan 5		Xmas Day observed.	
	Jan 6		Training	
HERZEELE	Jan 7		Bn was relieved by 23rd Manchesters & went to Billets south of HERZEELE. The Bn moved by train to PROVEN thence by light railway to HERZEELE. Billets in farm houses and barns. These were good but crowded and very scattered	
	Jan 8		Training in vicinity of billets.	
	Jan 9		do do	
	Jan 10		do do	
	Jan 11		do hymns	
	Jan 12		Brigade Parade at HOUTKERQUE for presentation of ribbons by Lieut Gen. Jacobs commanding II Corps	

Page 2.

Army Form C. 2118.

WAR DIARY
or
INTELLIGENCE SUMMARY.

(Erase heading not required.)

Place	Date	Hour	Summary of Events and Information	Remarks and references to Appendices
HERZEELE	1918 Jan 14		Training in vicinity of billets. Lt. Col. S. Chart returned from leave which over command of the Bn. from Major C. Hardy DSO	
	Jan 15		Training in vicinity of billets	
	Jan 16		do do	
	Jan 17		do do	
	Jan 18		do do	
	Jan 19		do do	
	Jan 20		do do	
	Jan 21	8 pm	The Bn. left HERZEELE for LA NEUVILLE (CORBIE). Entrained light Railway HERZEELE	
		9 pm	Detrained PROVEN	
		12.30am	Entrained PROVEN	
		2 pm	Detrained VILLERS BRETONNEAUX. Marched to billets at LA NEUVILLE.	
	Jan 22		Company & Platoon Training	
	Jan 30 midnight		Arrived 12 officers and 205 Other Ranks from 1/12th Bn. London Regt. At midnight on Jan 30/31 the style of the Battalion was changed from "2/12th Bn The London Regiment" to "12th Bn The London Regiment".	

Chris Hardy
Major